FOR I AM CONVINCED THAT NEITHER DEATH NOR LIFE, NEITHER ANGELS NOR DEMONS, NEITHER THE PRESENT NOR THE FUTURE, NOR ANY POWERS, NEITHER HEIGHT NOR DEPTH, NOR ANYTHING ELSE IN ALL CREATION, WILL BE ABLE TO SEPARATE US FROM THE LOVE OF GOD THAT IS IN CHRIST JESUS OUR LORD. (ROM. 8:38–39)

The AGAPE Love of God

Discover the True Meaning of Christian Life

Akwasi Afriyie

THE AGAPE LOVE OF GOD
Copyright © 2008 Akwasi Afriyie

ISBN-13: 978-1-897373-60-6
ISBN-10: 1-897373-60-0

All rights reserved. No part of this publication may be reproduced, stored in a retrieval system, or transmitted in any form or by any means—electronic, mechanical, photocopying, recording, or any other—except for brief quotations in printed reviews, without the prior written consent of the copyright owner or publisher. Any unauthorized publication is an infringement of the copyright law.

Scripture taken from the HOLY BIBLE, NEW INTERNATIONAL VERSION®. Copyright © 1973, 1978, 1984 International Bible Society. Used by permission of Zondervan. All rights reserved.

Printed by Word Alive Press
131 Cordite Road, Winnipeg, MB R3W 1S1
www.wordalivepress.ca

I DEDICATE THIS BOOK TO MY LOVELY
MOTHER, ANNA SERWAAH,
AND MY FATHER, EVANS A. PREMPEH,
WHO HAS BEEN A TRUE PATRIACH IN
THE FAMILY.

TO MY SISTERS NANA, MAVIS, AND
KATHLEEN—LOVE ALWAYS.

LIFE—Love is a way of life

OMNIPRESENT—Love is everywhere at the same time

VICTORY—Love conquers everything

EVERLASTING—Love is forevermore

TABLE OF CONTENTS

Preface		xi
Acknowledgments		xiii
Introduction		xv
Chapter 1:	God Is Love	1
Chapter 2:	God's Love vs. Human Love	13
Chapter 3:	The Law of Love	35
Chapter 4:	Emotions	43
Chapter 5:	The Power of Words	53
Chapter 6:	What Is Faith?	65
Chapter 7:	Faith through Love	73
Chapter 8:	Types of Love	79
Chapter 9:	Jesus, Our Example	89
Chapter 10:	Divine Love	95
Conclusion:	Mindset	103
Selected References		105
About The Author		107

—Akwasi Abayie

PREFACE

I'm really excited that God has placed this revelation of love in my heart.

The teaching of the Word of God inspired me to write this book and I'm convinced that after reading this book, it will become the number one book on your bookshelf. This book must be read with an open mind, an open heart, and with understanding in order to capture the practical meaning of God's agape love. All my life I have been missing the mark; I thought I was walking in the love of God, not knowing that I was only operating in selfishness. I thank God for enlightening my knowledge of his love and giving me the opportunity to share this truth with people from all walks of life.

I pray that your life and the lives of your families and friends will be transformed as you journey with this book. May God richly bless you as you read this book.

Glory be to God!

~Akwasi Afriyie

ACKNOWLEDGMENTS

First and foremost, I would like to thank Almighty God for inspiring me to write this book; without him it wouldn't have been possible. A big applause goes to my parents and sisters for believing in me and for supporting me every step of the way, God bless them. A special thanks to Pastor Charles Agyekum Fosu, for all his guidance, instruction, and his teaching of the Word of God. All the members of (ICC) International Charismatic Church—thank you for your love and support—you know who you are. I can't forget all the friends and family that encouraged me through this journey: Poly Bhari, Michael Prempeh Agyemang, Alex Oppong, Owen Oshodin, Lee Mohammed, Clement Aboagye-Mensah, Anthony Bill McDermott, Andre Hetherington, Samuel Opoku Agyemang, Raymond Odame Gyima, Ellen Minta Koduah, and Colleen McKenna. A big thanks goes to anybody that I may have forgotten to mention; you have a place in my heart.

INTRODUCTION

The love of God is the power of God because God is love and love produces power. Jesus was filled with compassion and, out of compassion, he was able to heal the sick, raise the dead, and turn five loaves of bread and two fish into dinner for five thousand people.

Many Christians today are seeking faith, power, healing, deliverance, peace, and prosperity, but have left behind the root to the entire power source—love, the essence of Christianity.

- We are commanded by God Almighty to love one another as he loves us.

- In order for us to demonstrate that we love God, we have to love the brothers and sisters we are in contact with every day.

- Almighty God created this universe based on the compassion within his heart.

- Walking in love will free you from any law dealing with sin and death because God is love and love never fails.

- Religion has trained us to love conditionally, but God says we are obligated to love unconditionally.

The agape love of God should be the number one priority in every Christian's life. We have to decide to walk in God's agape love so we can start seeing its manifestation in every area of our lives. I'm delighted that this book will bring to light the things that we have missed and then transform our lives so that we will never be the same.

Glory be to God Almighty. Hallelujah!

Chapter 1

GOD IS LOVE

What an awesome God we serve! He is able to outlast all our iniquities and still have a capacity of love for us. We tend to run away from God and the church the moment we sin, but God runs after us to save us from diving deep into sin. Self-consciousness has deceived us into thinking that God does not want to have anything to do with us. He is always at the scene to forgive us but we fail to yield to him. We shouldn't allow fear to grasp us to the point where we don't even ask to be forgiven.

According to Gen. 3:8–9, after Adam and Eve disobeyed God in the Garden of Eden, he called unto them; he didn't walk away from them. In fact, God even made garments for them to wear to cover their nakedness (3:21).

AGAPE LOVE OF GOD

Agape in the Greek language means unconditional and eternal love—*The God kind of love*. Agape is a spiritual love expressed by God to his children. It is a love without boundaries. It is a selfless love. The verb form of the word is *agapao*.

John 3:16–17 reads:

> *For God so loved [agapao] the world that he gave his one and only Son, that whoever believes in him shall not perish but have eternal life. For God did not send his Son into the world to condemn the world, but to save the world through him.*

"*So* loved" helps us understand that God's love for the sinful world is earnest and sincere, desiring all to be saved.

Ever since the fall of man in the beginning, mankind was distant from God and deep into sin. God used many great prophets such as Isaiah, Daniel, Jeremiah, and Elijah to preach his word and change lives. Evidently, sin was still erupting in the world, and God made a decision to send his only begotten Son to conquer sin and death so we do not have to be in bondage to sin, but free from sin. The only way to reconcile with God was through the precious blood of Jesus Christ on Calvary.

It is not God's will that anyone should perish but that everyone should have eternal life. However, some people have positioned themselves to perish by disregarding the salvation given to us.

Deut. 30:19 reads:

This day I call Heaven and earth as witness against you that I have set before you life and death, blessings and curses. Now choose life, so that you and your children may live.

Life is full of decision-making. For instance, every day people are making decisions about whom to marry, which vehicle to drive, which school to attend, and which food to consume. The decisions we make will bring us to our final destination. God is not demanding that we obey his commandments; he has rested the decision on us. If you are ignorant, he said to choose life so that you will live and not die.

Matt. 7:9–11 reads:

Which of you, if his son asks for bread, will give him a stone? Or if he asks for a fish, will give him a snake? If you, then, though you are evil, know how to give good gifts to your children, how much more will your Father in Heaven give good gifts to those who ask him!

"Evil" means morally bad or wrong; something that causes harm or distress. Jesus says even mere men, evil in their ways trained in human love and whose love is governed by emotions, are capable of giving good gifts to their children. How much more will your Heavenly Father, who created you and knows what your needs are, give to you when you ask!

God is able to do exceedingly more than what we can think or ask for. We should not underestimate God and make him so small that we can hardly see him.

The bigger you make God, the bigger he will be at the scene of your life—the smaller you make God the smaller he will be at the scene of your life!

GOD'S LOVE

Gen. 1:1 reads:

In the beginning God created the Heavens and the earth.

First of all, God's motives for creating this world were based on the love that he possesses. There would not have been any creation if no love existed within him. In other words, God, who *is* love, was motivated *by* love to create this world. The faithful words that he spoke into existence were an act of his love, and now we are living in the manifestation of what he spoke. God's agape love produced God's faith, and creation began. God's faith is carried by God's love; love is the energizing force behind faith.

Gen. 1:26 reads:

Then God said, "Let us make man in our image, in our likeness, and let them rule over the fish of the sea and the birds of the air, over the livestock, over all the earth, and over all the creatures that move along the ground."

Mankind was created in the image and the likeness of God (an exact duplicate of God). God is a spirit, therefore man is a spirit; he lives in a physical body and he possesses a soul. God is love, and since we were created in his image and likeness, we will automatically be of love, just like he is love. In other words, we were given the same personality traits as God when he created us. We were originally created with the tendency to love one another just as God loves us, but we have covered up and buried that love to a point where it no longer shows among us.

When a couple gets together and has a baby, the baby comes out having the features of the father and/or the mother. The baby's various personality traits will be similar to either one of the parents.

In Rom. 5:5 we read:

And hope does not disappoint us, because God has poured out his love into our hearts by the Holy Spirit, whom he has given us.

God says our hope will not disappoint us. How?

God poured out his agape love into our hearts by the Holy Spirit the very day we accepted Jesus Christ as our Lord and Saviour. The substance needed for faith to work is hope—no hope, no faith. When hope is present, it will give substance for faith to work. But faith will not work without love, because love is the power that turns on our faith. The love within us is the force that supports our faith so it can work.

God has already poured his heavenly agape love into our hearts so we can be capable of loving others like he loves us. We should be able to walk in supernatural love. There is no excuse for Christians to say, "I tried to love others but it's too difficult. I want to love, but I just can't."

If pressure is not applied to the flesh while you are cultivating love, then how can you mature in love? You will not be able to see the level where your love walk can reach. We must develop and train ourselves in God's agape love or else we will fail to resist temptation. We have to start by loving ourselves and the people in our households, and then we can direct that same love towards others. By the same token, charity begins at home. The word love originated from charity. Charity is love in action.

1 John 4:16 reads:

And so we know and rely on the love God has for us. God is Love. Whoever lives in love lives in God, and God in him.

The Bible tells us that *God is love.* God does not manufacture love, he does not pretend to love, he doesn't *have* love, he *is* love. When we see love in the scripture, that means God, and where there is love there is God, because God is love. Somehow, certain people perceive the truth differently and conclude that "God *has* love." He certainly does, but that is not the whole truth.

Love × Love = God. In mathematics, multiplying 1 × 1 always equals 1. God's love is infinite.

God is the definition of love. There is absolutely nothing that can surpass the love that God has for us.

Without God's love abounding in us we would not be able to sustain life by ourselves. We rely on God's love whether we are aware of it or not. We rely on God's sun for energy, God's air to breathe into our body, and God's water to quench our thirst.

Whoever lives in love lives in God, and God in him.

Likewise, selfishness is the opposite of love. Whoever lives in selfishness lives in Satan, and Satan in him or her. The root of all *sin* is based on selfishness, and selfishness is of the devil. Where sin exists, selfishness will be present, because people are concerned about self-preservation, about their own needs being met, and not thinking about others.

LOVE LIKE A MOUNTAIN

God's love is more meaningful than the simple human phrase "I love you." Humans tend to use that phrase interchangeably based on emotions that can range from lust to mere affection. These three words do not spell love. An action speaks louder than words. God expresses his love through actions, and not just words.

God's love is similar to a mountain. A mountain stands firm from season to season, year to year, day to day, and still remains unchanged. Mountains are not moved by weather conditions such as snowstorms, sun, rain, or clouds—they always stand on their guard.

God's love is not moved by the numerous sins we may commit or the kinds of sins we may commit. His arms are always ready to forgive and accept us.

THE GREATEST COMMANDMENT

What is love? Love is an expression of your character.
Matt. 22:37–40 reads:

> "Love the Lord your God with all your heart and with all your soul and with all your mind." "This is the first and greatest commandment. And the second is like it: "Love your neighbor as yourself." All the Law and the Prophets hang on these two commandments.

How can we love God?

Loving God is not going to church, it is not ushering at the church, it is not singing in the choir, it is not playing an instrument in the church, it is not doing things for the church. However, these things are evidently wonderful to do as a child of God because they display our passion for Christ.

To love God is to obey his commandments and to love our neighbours as ourselves—to love even our enemies as ourselves.

Who are our neighbours?

A neighbour is any person that we come into contact with in our day-to-day lives. They could be black, white, brown, or yellow; from different parts of the world; or of different races, different cultures, and different languages. We can't just display love towards the people in our own ethnic group and culture.

Love is not based on colour, for it is colourless. Love is a reflection of God's beautiful rainbow; it has all the colours a painter would need to finish his or her task. A rainbow is not prejudiced against colour because it is full of colours, and that's how our love should be—without prejudice toward any colour.

Love is from the heart; anything else is selfishness. When we try to love others with our mind or emotions, we are only making judgments as to whether or not we should really love that person. But when sincere love is flowing from our hearts, we will love others without thinking about it.

Love your neighbour as yourself—there is no possible way to love your neighbour if you can't first love yourself. The way you feel about yourself will likely reflect how you feel about somebody else.

Certain individuals put themselves down until they have no more confidence. They think they are the biggest losers, never amounting to anything, so they walk around with low self-esteem and feelings of "I'm not pretty enough," or "I'm not handsome enough."

However, God took time to form and create us. He made us the way we are as a blessing for somebody else. True beauty comes from within, and not without, our outward appearance cannot match our inner beauty.

According to the Bible, there are two spiritual laws opposing each other: the Law of the Spirit of Life in Christ Jesus and the Law of Sin and Death. Every individual on the face of this earth is living under one of these two laws whether they are aware of it or not. They will work for either advantage or disadvantage, for the law by which you live will gradually bring you to your destination. To walk in the Spirit is to walk in love and to be led by the Spirit of God. If we walk in the Spirit, our desires will be governed by the Spirit, as will our thoughts, our mindset, and our character.

If we walk by the sinful nature, our thoughts, our mindset, and our character will be governed by the sinful nature. Almighty God is pleased when we walk in the Spirit (love). The devil is happy when we walk in the sinful nature (selfishness).

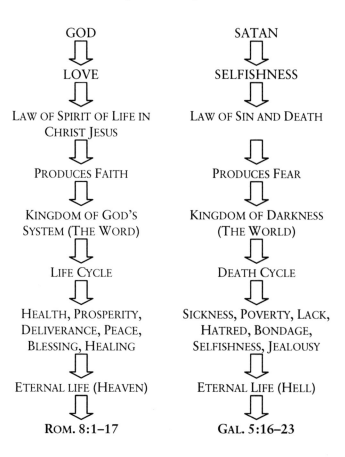

GOD	SATAN
⇩	⇩
LOVE	SELFISHNESS
⇩	⇩
LAW OF SPIRIT OF LIFE IN CHRIST JESUS	LAW OF SIN AND DEATH
⇩	⇩
PRODUCES FAITH	PRODUCES FEAR
⇩	⇩
KINGDOM OF GOD'S SYSTEM (THE WORD)	KINGDOM OF DARKNESS (THE WORLD)
⇩	⇩
LIFE CYCLE	DEATH CYCLE
⇩	⇩
HEALTH, PROSPERITY, DELIVERANCE, PEACE, BLESSING, HEALING	SICKNESS, POVERTY, LACK, HATRED, BONDAGE, SELFISHNESS, JEALOUSY
⇩	⇩
ETERNAL LIFE (HEAVEN)	ETERNAL LIFE (HELL)
⇩	⇩
ROM. 8:1–17	GAL. 5:16–23

Chapter 2

GOD'S LOVE VS. HUMAN LOVE

CONTRAST BETWEEN GOD'S LOVE AND HUMAN LOVE

Dear friends, let us love one another, for love comes from God. Everyone who loves has been born of God and knows God. Whoever does not love does not know God, because God is love. (1 John 4:7–8)

God's agape love is supernatural—it comes directly from God himself.

We must adopt the God kind of love because it is not from this world's system. The only way people can identify that we are born into the family of God is if our lives are characterized by love. We can talk about how much we love God, how much we read the scriptures, and how much knowledge we have gained from the scriptures; however, the Bible says if we don't put that love into practice, then we are only assuming that we love God. However, we don't intimately know God, for God is love.

God's love does not need to be loved in order to express love. It continues to love no matter what the circumstances may be. God's love is not prejudiced. This type of love is able to endure the rain, the pain, and the pressures of life. God's love is higher then any height, deeper than any depth, wider than any width, longer than any length, and stronger than death itself. We have to first walk in this kind of love to be able to comprehend it. Moreover, this love was there in the beginning and it will still be there at the end of the ages. It is the measure of everything.

Characteristics of God's Love:

God's Love has a Satisfaction Guarantee

You can count on God's love in your darkest hour. He will never fail you, even though your friends and family may fail you. How many people do you know that you can genuinely count on in times of hardship? God will never give up on us, but we tend to give up on him due to our circumstances.

When you purchase an item from the store and the seller provides you with a five year warranty, if the item happens to break down, they are bound by the rules and regulations set in that warranty to change, replace, or fix the item. Likewise, God will also keep his promises and commandments, but can we keep his Word in order for him to do what he says he will do?

Num. 23:19 reads:

God is not a man, that he should lie, nor a son of man, that he should change his mind. Does he speak and then not act? Does he promise and not fulfill?

God's Love is Unconditional
The Bibles tells us in Matt. 5:45b,

He causes his sun to rise on the evil and the good, and sends rain on the righteous and the unrighteous.

God's love does not come with a price tag—it is free and it will set you free to love others. God has already set himself up to forgive us even before we sin. He is not waiting on our love before he will respond with his love back to us. God's love is the common denominator in our lives; it never changes even though we humans (the numerators) always change.

God's Love is One-Sided
God's love is like a one-way street: always flowing the same direction—toward us! He will continue to love when it is good, when it is bad, and when it is

difficult to love. Moreover, he will continue to give when he has to give and when he does not have to give, and he does not anticipate the same favour in return. There is absolutely nothing we can ever do for God to stop loving us. He has committed himself to loving this world regardless.

God's Love is Others-Centred

God's love is unselfish. It seeks good and privilege for others without any regard to self. It is not concerned about "me, myself, and I" because it is priceless. God's attention is not on himself, his attention is on us and he desires that we draw our attention to others. Our horizontal relationship with others will determine the effectiveness of our vertical relationship with the Father. Perfecting our love walk with others will ultimately perfect our love walk with God.

HUMAN LOVE

Mankind's understanding of love is different from what God's agape love means. From infancy and through the early stages of our childhood, we have not been taught to walk in the agape love of God. Instead, we have been practicing religious doctrines about the ways of love along with the trends society has set in place.

Real love is what God is all about, not the ways of this world. God has introduced his agape love to us because of our inability to love others like he does. Human love is an emotional and conditional type of love based on carnality. Our degree of love does not measure up to anything. The devil has deceived us where our love walk is concerned, for now "love" is universally used to define and describe many things *except* its original purpose. Human love is limited, cold-hearted, and selfish, and it is turned on and off by emotions.

Love should be a way of life, the reason for our existence!

Characteristics of Human Love:

Human Love is Selfish
Isa. 14:12–15 reads:

> *How you have fallen from Heaven, O morning star, son of the dawn! You have been cast down to the earth, you who once laid low the nations! You said in your heart, "I will ascend to heaven; I will raise my throne above the stars of God; I will sit enthroned on the mount of assembly, on the utmost heights of the sacred mountain. I will ascend above the tops of the clouds; I will make myself like the Most High." But you are brought down to the grave, to the depths of the pit.*

Now we have a vivid picture of where selfishness originated from: Lucifer himself. As a result of his selfishness, sin was brought forth into the world. Selfishness is consumed with "me, myself, and I." (Notice how many times Lucifer said "I.") Lucifer was filled with pride, jealous ambition, and boastfulness. He exalted himself before God and, as a result, he was cast down from heaven.

Selfishness is seeking one's own desires or interests without any regard for others. We tend to preserve our own needs first, and in so doing, our love becomes limited towards others' needs. On the other hand, agape love is not concerned about "self" but about others. The centre of agape love is someone else. Our love should be focused on others so that God can focus on us.

We understand that selfishness is of the devil. Whenever "me, myself, and I" comes first, self-preservation will show up. But as Christians, we don't want to be of the devil (selfishness), we want to be of God (love). We have to make an effort to lay down our lives for others just as Christ Jesus laid down his life for us.

Human Love is Conditional

Just as human life goes through a cycle of change, human love reacts in like kind. Human love is based on a carnal state of mind. It expresses itself through feelings and thoughts. It allows the flesh to dictate its actions instead of letting the agape love of God take control. This type of conditional love cannot be relied on because it will only love when it is convenient to do so promptly.

Human Love as Boomerang

Human love is sort of like a "catch game." Human love says, *"I'm going to love you, and I expect you to reciprocate that same love back to me or else I won't love you any more."* This type of love is concerned about the benefits it will receive as a result of loving others. In other words, this love comes with a price tag that must be certified.

Human Love as "Price Tag"

Human love comes with a price tag that one must qualify for in order to be loved. A "price tag love" says, *"I will lend to you because you also lend to me; I will buy for you because you bought for me."* This type of love categorizes specific kinds of people it will love and do things together with. A person who loves with a price tag will always pick and choose who to love and how to love.

The characteristics of love are thus also subject to love. We cannot cultivate one area of love, such as kindness, and not have patience as well. If we do that, we will be missing some of the pieces to the puzzle. Generally speaking, we cannot have a whole pie if one quarter of it is missing. It's like a tree with many branches. The love is the root that supports the whole tree so it can stand firmly. The tree can be amputated, but the roots (love) will always produce a new tree. Our love walk can be challenged, mistreated, stepped on, walked over, and crushed down; yet we should always be courageous to get up and love others again with a fresh love. We are under a commandment to love, and challenges like these should not determine whether or not we should love.

SEEDTIME AND HARVESTTIME

Eccl. 11:1 reads:

Cast your bread upon the waters, for after many days you will find it again.

Everything in the kingdom of God is operated by faith, faith is operated by love, and these two principles operate under the law of seedtime and harvest. Jesus said in Luke 8:11 that the Word of God is a seed, and the seed of the Word of God is an incorruptible or imperishable seed. Then 1 Pet. 1:23 further describes a seed that will never fail to bring forth a harvest. A farmer understands that when he plants an apple seed, in due season he will reap a harvest. The Bible says we will reap what we sow, so in a nutshell, if you are sowing trouble, it is just a matter of time before you reap trouble and vice versa—if you are sowing humility, it is just a matter of time before you reap humility.

These attributes of love are excellent seeds to sow in the kingdom of God that will reap a full harvest. Walking in the agape love of God will not be in vain because God meant it for our benefit. Just as a farmer sows seeds and reaps a harvest, when we sow love we will reap the harvest of love in due season. When we cast our "bread"—our kindness, hope, patience, and trust—upon the waters, it might take a day, a week, a month, a year, or even years, but God says we are going to find it again.

THE ATTRIBUTES OF LOVE

1 Cor. 13:4–8

- God, who is Love, is Patient.
- God, who is Love, is Kind.
- God, who is Love, does not Envy.
- God, who is Love, is not Proud.
- God, who is Love, is not Rude.
- God, who is Love, is not Self-Seeking.
- God, who is Love, is not easily Angered.
- God, who is Love, keeps no record of wrongs.
- God, who is Love, does not delight in evil but rejoices with the truth.
- God, who is Love, always Protects.
- God, who is Love, always Trusts.

- God, who is Love, always Hopes.
- God, who is Love, always Perseveres.
- God, who is Love, never fails because God is Love.

VERSUS

- Mankind, who is selfish, is Impatient.
- Mankind, who is selfish, is Unkind.
- Mankind, who is selfish, is Envious.
- Mankind, who is selfish, is always Proud.
- Mankind, who is selfish, is Rude.
- Mankind, who is selfish, is always Self-Seeking.
- Mankind, who is selfish, is easily Angered.
- Mankind, who is selfish, always keeps record of wrongs.
- Mankind, who is selfish, delights in evil and does not rejoice with the truth.
- Mankind, who is selfish, seldom Protects.
- Mankind, who is selfish, seldom Trusts.
- Mankind, who is selfish, seldom Hopes.
- Mankind, who is selfish, seldom Perseveres.
- Mankind, who is selfish, always fails because mankind is Selfish.

Love is Patient

Patient refers to the ability or willingness to remain consistently or constantly the same.

Rom. 8:25 reads:

But if we hope for what we do not yet have, we wait for it patiently.

When we hope for something, we need to exercise patience in times of affliction to be able to persevere. This does not mean we will not have what we are hoping for. But maybe we aren't ready for what we are hoping for, or what we hope for might not be ready to give birth to what we desire. If we fail to exercise patience in our request, we might miss out on God's best for our lives. Our faith requires patience in order to manifest. God is extraordinarily patient towards us all the time.

We have all heard the old sayings "Patience is a virtue" and "Good things come to those who wait." These phrases are true because they are based on true facts that occurred at a particular time. In our daily lives we have to exercise patience for certain events to take place. For instance, we have to exercise patience for our mechanic to fix our car, or we have to wait in line at other public facilities.

David says in Ps. 40:1,

I waited patiently for the Lord; he turned to me and heard my cry.

Love is Kind
Kindness is the quality of being warm-hearted, considerate, humane and sympathetic toward others.

Kindness is the door our goodness can flow out through. When we show kindness by love, the recipient person receives goodness as an act of our kindness. As believers, our kindness towards unbelievers moves them in the direction of seeking after our God. Kindness is like salt; no matter how you shake it, it will always produce the same flavour. It is polite to hold the door for the person behind you. It shows a sign of respect to reserve your seat for the elderly or somebody that needs it more than you do.

Love does Not Envy
Envy is a feeling of discomfort caused by the prosperity of another.

Jealousy is a spirit that can make you belittle your self-worth as you compare yourself to others. Jealous and envious people view someone else's success as a threat to their own success. They tend to have hard feelings whenever preference is shown to someone else, even to the point of ill will towards that person.

For example, God blesses an individual with a new vehicle and a beautiful house. Instead of his or her friends and family rejoicing together, they respond with unkind remarks about the goodness of God.

God says in Rom. 12:15,

Rejoice with those who rejoice; mourn with those who mourn.

We should learn to rejoice and praise God together whenever our brothers or sisters in Christ receive an increase or favour from God. When jealous ambition is not managed or controlled, it can leave a loophole leading to the unthinkable.

Love is Not Proud

Pride is feeling pleasurable satisfaction over an act, possession, or quality.

"*God opposes the proud but gives grace to the humble,*" James 4:6b. A prideful person will establish his or her own downfall. When we boast of our self-worth, we limit God, who made everything possible. Some people have the idea that everything they own came into their possession by their own strength and ability. If we want to boast about anything, it should be about Christ and his resurrection. Pride is an act of selfishness. A person with a proud spirit carries the image of Lucifer. Lucifer was full of himself and proceeded with selfish ambition.

The Bible says,

- God . . . hates pride and arrogance. (Prov. 8:13)

- God . . . opposes the proud. (James 4:6)

- God . . . is distant from the proud. (Ps. 138:6)

- God . . . will bring down the proud. (Isa. 25:11)

The Consequences of Pride:

- Pride will result in . . . shame (Prov. 11:2)
- Pride will result in . . . destruction and downfall (Prov. 16:18)
- Pride will result in . . . being brought low (Prov. 29:23)
- Pride will result in . . . being deceived. (Obad. 1:3)
- Pride will result in . . . being hardened of heart (Ex. 5:2)
- Pride will result in . . . being conceited (1 Tim. 6:3–4)

Overcoming Pride:

- Humble yourself before God. (James 4:10)
- Trust God and do not lean on your own understanding. (Prov. 3:5–7)
- Do not think highly of yourself. (Rom. 12:3)
- Honour one another above yourself. (Rom. 12:10)
- Let love take root in your heart, and stay free from pride and selfishness.

Love is Not Rude
To be rude is to lack refinement or social skills.

The socially incorrect behaviour of rudeness is an attribute every individual despises to be addressed with. An unseemly and unpleasant behaviour creates enemies. In others words, a rude or moody attitude only builds an atmosphere of adversity around you.

It is absolutely civilized to greet people kindly. It is an act of character to respond to people in a humane manner by responding with "Thank you," "I beg your pardon," "Please," "Excuse me," or "Sorry." We cannot wear our hearts on our sleeves about what someone else did to us. *Our attitude in life will always determine our aptitude in life.*

Love is Not Self-Seeking
Self-Seeking is to preserve one's interest or advantage.

Agape love is not self-seeking, but rather, others-seeking. When we seek our own advantage over others' advantage, we allow ourselves to operate in selfishness. But when we are able to seek benefits and advantages for others, God provides benefits and advantages for us. Some people figure that it's a dog-eat-dog world, so they just look out for themselves and their family. But we can always be more considerate and conscious of our surroundings.

Love is not easily Angered
Anger is a strong feeling of displeasure aroused by an act done to another.

A mature person will not be offended when someone provokes them to lose their joy. There are millions of things that can cause one to lose their joy, but it takes maturity not to react or be offended.

Anger can be as deadly as a murder weapon when it is not managed. The first thing that rings a bell in an angered mind is evil over good instead of good over evil. The Bible says in Ps. 30:5 that *God's anger only lasts for a moment.* We ought to adopt God's nature, as anger is part of our make-up. We have to be aware of the enemy's tactics to be able to withstand his works against us. We don't have to attend anger management classes or get assigned to anger specialists in order to deal with our anger.

Eph. 4:26 says,

"In your anger do not sin." Do not let the sun go down while you are still angry.

Love Does Not Keep a Record of Wrongs

Wrong is defined as contrary to the principles of justice or law.

When God forgives our sins, he does not keep an account or a remembrance of them (Heb. 8:12). Well, it is not that he forgets about it, but more that he's not interested in keeping a record of it. Thus, he is interested in seeing the better you. And yet, some Christians find pleasure in retrieving the stories from another's past (before they became born again) and making them the news of the week. We each have to realize that our past was not all that great before we were saved. The Bible reminds us in Rom. 3:23 that *"all have sinned and fall short of the glory of God."*

The Bible says that Lucifer is the accuser of many brethren (Rev. 12:10). In other words, he stands before God and prosecutes each one of us according to our conduct. However, God simply lets the accusation go in one ear and out the other.

Love Does Not Delight in Evil but Rejoices with the Truth
Truth is the thing that corresponds to fact or reality.

A person full of love will not take offence from not being the candidate for a job or the leader of a club, but will rejoice with the truth. Love does not entertain the downfall of others, but rejoices in the prosperity of others. Since love always seeks good for others, it can never rejoice when evil prevails. Yet, there are people who endure great joy to see their enemies in agony, defeated and crying for help. It ought not to be that way; the Bible says we should choose good over evil.

Love Always Protects
To protect is to prevent somebody or something from being harmed or damaged.

When an oasis of love is ruling in our heart, it will enable us to say to a friend, "These people might be making negative remarks about you but I'm not going to join in. I'm going to be that friend who will remain loyal to you and protect you from harm." It assures a child to know that his or her parents are available regardless of any mess they might get themselves involved in. Lastly, it releases stress for a husband or wife when one becomes the centre of a mishap. Love always protects, not only when it is convenient to do so. We ought to protect our loved ones by staying close, believing in them, and encouraging them whenever they encounter afflictions.

Love Always Trusts

Trust is a reliance on the integrity, veracity, or reliability of a person or thing.

It's truly understandable that it's not as easy as it seems to regain trust toward someone after they have thrown their trustworthiness out the window. However, we can always give them the benefit of the doubt by reconstructing our thoughts and heart attitudes towards them. We have to learn not to set our expectations so high, or else we will always end up being the one that gets hurt. Our level of trust will either continue to grow or fade as we learn more about a person, but in the end, we have to realize that people are always going to be people. They will let you down one way or another. But nevertheless, with love and forgiveness we can always rebuild our trust with accountability for change.

I have heard some people say that they don't trust anybody but God, and there are others who don't trust anybody but themselves. If we see clearly, we fail to trust ourselves when we fail to follow up on our own words. You might wonder why one would make such a statement. Most of the time, it ends up that one pours out their heart to a dear friend only to be betrayed. If you were to think of trust and money in the same category, when someone vulnerably puts his or her trust in someone else, it's sort of like they are putting their life's fortune into that person's hands, believing positively that it will be safe. In the end, the only way for us not to be hurt is to put our trust and hope in God, for he will never fail or be disloyal to us. True security of trust can be discovered in God, where it will not be forfeited.

Love Always Hopes
Hope is the belief that something desirable will happen or be possible.

Hope is not just having our head above the clouds, and it is far from just positive thinking. It is a pattern of optimistic perseverance until changes are seen in one's life or circumstances. Hope is needful to set the grounds for our faith. We all have hope for changes in the future concerning our lives and the world we live in. For instance, we go to school hoping to acquire a good job. Also, we might participate in a gambling activity with the hope of winning. But without hope, we fail to strive for change. Our hope sets the course for what we desire to achieve, and for as long as we live we will always have hope in something or someone. Hope keeps us going, compared to fear, which keeps us paralyzed instead of reaching for what we desire or believe in. Fear actually becomes a false hope.

Love Always Perseveres
Perseverance is steady and continued action or belief, usually over a long period and especially despite difficulties or setbacks.

When push comes to shove, it's not time for us to give up and lose hope, but rather, to rise up and soar above those obstacles. You may be wondering, "Why am I facing all these problems even though I'm a born again Christian?" First of all, trouble is inevitable; as long as we live in this world, we will face trouble. But according to James 1:12, *"Blessed is the man who perseveres under trial, because when he has stood the test, he will receive the crown of life that God has promised to those who love him."*

If we are not able to persevere through trials and tribulations, we will not be able to receive the crown of life from God. These challenges come in order to strengthen us and build up our trust and confidence in the Lord.

Love Never Fails
To fail is to be unsuccessful in trying to do something.

Have you ever thought about why love never fails? Well, it's because God is love and he can't fail. He is like a doctor who has never lost a patient. He's like a lawyer who has never lost a case. He is the God who always keeps his promises. There is neither failure in him now nor any that we are aware of from the time-line of this world. He honours his Word above all things in creation. In fact, the Bible let's us know that *"His Word will never return to him empty, but accomplish what he desires and achieve the purpose for which he sent it"* (Isa. 55:11). We can rest assured that with God all things are possible if only we believe. It is time for Christians to place their trust and confidence in the Lord instead of in self, family, and friends. There are times when people may be reluctant to assist us in times of need, but God is available for us 24–7, 365-days-a-year.

Chapter 3

THE LAW OF LOVE

WHAT IS A LAW?

A law is an established principle set in place to be followed by society and enforced by law authorities.

But the fruit of the Spirit is love, joy, peace, patience, kindness, goodness, faithfulness, gentleness and self-control. Against such things there is no law. (Gal. 5:22–23)

Laws affect everyone in society, including the lawmakers, and they impact our standard of living. Virtually every person is a potential victim until they violate the law. Laws are important, for they ensure the safety of our environment and, most importantly, a better world. Without laws set in place, the world would be out of control and in chaos.

Furthermore, natural laws originated from spiritual laws, yet we tend to put more emphasis on natural laws. This is evident in the sense that a lawbreaker will face immediate consequences when breaking natural laws, while spiritual laws take action when a person dies or sets their own doom.

The law of love is the law of the New Covenant or the Law of Jesus. It supersedes any other law you may have heard of either in the spiritual or physical realm. It surpasses the law of sin, the Law of Moses, the law of faith, the law of attraction, the law of gravity, and other human laws. If there is such thing as an "eternal law," it is the law of love because God is love and he is eternal.

The fruit of the Spirit is love, and when we develop and are perfected in love, it will produce in us such excellent attributes such joy, peace, patience, kindness, goodness, faithfulness, gentleness, and self-control. Everything that we anticipate from God hangs on the law of love, such as answered prayer and forgiveness for our confessions. We have to awaken the areas of our love walk that have become dormant, for they play vital roles in our quality of life.

The law of faith works, but we often underestimate how well it will work for us. Likewise, the law of love works proficiently at all times, but we often fail to turn it on to operate it. In contrast to other laws that govern this natural world, we tend to believe in the law of faith and the law of love with a shadow of doubt. For instance, the law of gravity will work for anybody that gets involved in it. It is no respecter of persons. We firmly understand that if an object is tossed in the air, it will certainly drop down in a matter of seconds, and so, we will not jump off a building because we understand the consequences of that law. The only exception is when there is something able to resist gravity like an airplane, hot air balloon, or parachute.

LOVING YOUR ENEMIES

But I tell you who hear me: Love your enemies, do good to those who hate you, bless those who curse you, pray for those who mistreat you. (Luke 6:27–28)

The principle of love might seem weak to the eyes of the world, but it produces victory in the kingdom of God. Notice, God will never command his children to do something that will bring harm and danger into their lives. We ought to love our enemies just like Christ loved his enemies. Apparently, in the world it will be abnormal to *love your enemies and do good to those that hate you.* Let's keep in mind that Jesus is a prophet and he is making a provision for us to receive blessing when others mistreat us. But how are we going to receive blessing if we retaliate like the world? When we are able to love the unlovely, it will allow us to reach a level of spiritual maturity. During his earthly ministry, Jesus showed compassion to the Sadducees and Pharisees regardless of their false teaching against the Word of God. In spite all of the criticism, persecution, and curses our enemies may direct at us, our Lord desires for each of us to become the "big person" and respond by seeking their best interest. It is absolutely possible for us to love our enemies through Christ Jesus. When we make the effort, I believe God will give us the grace to overcome our weaknesses. It is very easy to love family and friends, but the real challenge is to love the people we dislike.

The world says to take revenge on your enemies; God says to love your enemies. Which one will you choose?

> *If someone strikes you on one cheek, turn to him the other also. If someone takes your cloak, do not stop him from taking your tunic. (Luke 6:29)*

Human nature is constantly concerned about self, which, many times, seems to limit the time we have to be concerned about others. Truthfully, it will take Christ-like character for us to seek others' best interest instead of our own. We have become accustomed to religious doctrines that lead us to react in the same manner as the world. Our carnal mind desires for us to retaliate, but God desires for us to go the extra mile even though others mistreat us. Supposedly, we ought to turn the other cheek because God has commanded us to do so. It is a choice; we can either honour God's Word and gain reward in heaven or seek our own way and gain reward from man.

Give to everyone who asks you, and if anyone takes what belongs to you, do not demand it back. Do to others as you would have them do to you. (Luke 6:30–31)

As Christians, we represent Christ here on earth, so we ought to be trendsetters rather than jumping onto the bandwagon like everybody else. The principles of God will work for us only if we can walk in them. Giving is not necessarily limited to money—we can give time, encouraging words or help to the needy. It is a form of sowing a seed in God's kingdom and reaping a harvest. As well, our giving shouldn't be reserved for only certain categories of individuals. Notice, Christ said, *"Give to everyone who asks you,"* which includes our enemies.

In my personal life, I used to chase and nag people simply because they had borrowed something that belonged to me. Then I came across this scripture: "*. . . if anyone takes what belongs to you, do not demand it back.*" It was not easy at first to refrain from claiming back my belongings; however, I was determined that if Jesus said not to demand it back, I would not demand it back. I believe that God is a God of justice and he will always restore our former goods. When we crown ourselves as gods and seek to enforce our rights, God is not able to intervene to bring justice in our situations.

Imagine what the world would be like today if all of us applied the principles of love in our daily lives. Division and poverty would be conquered and peace and positive human rights would be brought into the world. Our Lord commanded us to empathize with others. In other words, if we don't want nuisance at our dwelling, we shouldn't bring it to our neighbour's dwelling.

WHAT CREDIT?

> *If you love those who love you, what credit is that to you? Even "sinners" love those who love them. And if you do good to those who are good to you, what credit is that to you? Even "sinners" do that. And if lend to those from whom you expect repayment, what credit is that to you? Even "sinners" lend to "sinners," expecting to be repaid in full. (Luke 6:32–34)*

Christians are to be the "*salt of the world*" and "*the light of the world.*" But if the salt is unable to produce any flavour and our light cannot shine like the children of God, what credit will we earn? I mentioned early on that we are representatives of Christ. However, if there is no distinction between Christians and the world, how can we truly represent Christ? Likewise, if the Christian life is parallel to the world, what difference are we making in the world? Most people are aware of basic moral principles and the value of expressing goodwill to others, but there is always a limit to how far they will go. In contrast, Jesus wants believers to go the extra mile to meet their neighbour's needs without a limit. That's when we will be able to gain reward from above and become known as the children of God.

> *But love your enemies, do good to them, and lend to them without expecting to get anything back. Then your reward will be great, and you will be sons of the Most High, because he is kind to the ungrateful and wicked. Be merciful, just as your Father is merciful.*
> *(Luke 6:35–36)*

The law of love is the fulfillment of spiritual and natural laws. Instead of trying to keep the Ten Commandments, if we love God and love our neighbours as ourselves, we have fulfilled the law of love.

*Your faith can fail you,
but your love will never fail you!*

Chapter 4

EMOTIONS

WHAT ARE EMOTIONS? ☺

An emotion is a psychological change caused by the feeling of pain or pleasure and is expressed by your actions.

"You can't keep the birds from flying over your head, but you can keep them from building a nest on your head." Similary, we cannot change the Bible, so we might as well let the Bible change us. Emotions are inevitable; they come as results of our sensory mechanisms interacting with what we see, hear, feel, smell, and touch. We are going to encounter emotions as long as we live, so it only benefits us to discover ways of controlling them. Every person has a combination of positive and negative emotions that show up from time to time. Some of the positive emotions are joy, gratitude, and happiness. On the other hand, some of the negative emotions are fear, bitterness, jealousy, and anger. Men and women deal with emotions on extremely different levels. For instance, men tend to conceal their emotions while women will more often verbalize their emotions.

God created human beings with emotions. Man is a triune (three-part) being—he is a spirit, lives in a physical body, and possesses a soul. The soul is also made up of three components: mind, will and emotions. Our emotions determine the way we feel and are a crucial part of the soulish realm. Many cultures and religions have their own views of what the soul is all about. The soul is believed to be a self-aware essence unique to particular living beings. It is immortal and unseen by the human eyes. It is believed to be one of the avenues that bring forth a wellspring of wisdom.

The way you think (either according to the Word of God or to the world's ways) determines what types of emotions you will have.

Matt. 10:28 reads:

Do not be afraid of those who kill the body but cannot kill the soul. Rather, be afraid of the One who can destroy both soul and body in hell.

God makes it clear that the soul and the body are two different things and when a person dies their soul still lives. The soul is said to be absent from the body after death, returning back to God. It holds the true identity of an individual and it has the capability of restoring a person back to life.

People in different countries or from different cultures may portray emotions in different ways, yet emotions cannot be concealed even if we try, although there are individuals with naturally introverted or extroverted personality traits. Emotions are vital to our social existence.

Some of the commonly universally known basic emotions are:

- Joy
- Distress
- Fear
- Disgust
- Anger
- Surprise

Your emotions will lead you!

In 3 John 2 we read:

> *Dear friend, I pray that you may enjoy good health and that all may go well with you, even as your soul is getting along well.*

It is God's will for all believers to prosper in every area of their lives, including health and matters of the soul with regard to what they think, choose, and feel. If your soul (emotions) prospers then your entire life will also follow. Generally speaking, emotions will eventually affect your life, depending on how you deal with them, for better or for worse. The only intellectual way for us to rule over our emotions is to submit them to God's word. God gave us emotions to benefit our lives; he didn't mean for them to rule over our lives.

In Gen. 2:15–17 we read:

The Lord God took the man and put him in the Garden of Eden to work it and take care of it. And the Lord God commanded the man, "You are free to eat from any tree in the garden; but you must not eat of the knowledge of good and evil, for when you eat of it you will surely die."

Now, notice that God gave authority to Adam to control and maintain the Garden of Eden. Adam's emotions were not provoked to eat the fruit from the tree of the knowledge of good and evil. I believe that Adam saw the tree daily, walked around it and tended it like any of the other plants, that is, until Eve was deceived by Satan to eat of the fruit thereof and gave some to Adam to eat also. Let's notice that nobody has the power to control your emotions unless you give in to them.

In others words, without the Word of God residing in our heart producing positive emotions, our negative emotions will destroy us. The tree was not appealing to Adam until Eve brought it to his attention. Adam could have taken authority over his emotions by speaking faith-filled words, but he gave in to his emotions. Sometimes people try to talk you into doing things you were determined to abstain from and your emotions react to what they are suggesting. Whether your emotions are governed by the Word or by the world will determine the outcome. Adam's emotions became unstable when he heard Satan's words contradicting the Word of God, and this moved him away from the things of God.

We are all responsible for what we allow our minds to dwell on. If our thinking is in line with God's ways of doing things, then our emotions will follow as well. Likewise, if our thinking is in line with the world's ways of doing things, then our emotions will follow as well.

It is absolutely impossible to think in line with the Word and produce emotions of the things of the world. The Bible says that as a man thinks so is he (Prov. 23:7 KJV), therefore, we are products of the things we allow our minds to dwell on. Your thinking will produce the kinds of emotions that will be present in your life. The Word of God will produce godly emotions, and the word of the devil will produce worldly emotions.

Who are you listening to and making decision together with?

Overcoming Emotions

If we look at the origins of the word emotion, we see that its definition includes a sense of "motion," which means to be actively moving or changing in process. Our emotions are constantly playing a part in our lives, and in turn, we have to play our part to control them. God desires for us to have positive emotions, thus the devil desires for us to have negative emotions. The outcome of it all will either make you or break you. The more we gain a thorough understanding of emotions, the more we can acknowledge how they affect our lives. Even when we make rational decisions based on how we feel, there is still the possibility of regret. Nevertheless, individuals who do not control their own emotions will leave them in motion by controlling somebody else.

Jesus, the author and finisher of our faith, had emotions but they never had him. According to Mark 14:34, Jesus was overwhelmed with trouble and depressed. His soul was struck with terror to the point that it almost killed him. The intensity rose to the degree where Jesus' emotions were talking for him, for he said, "*Father . . . take this cup from me*" (v. 36). Although Jesus understood his mission and purpose on this earth was to gain salvation for all men, his emotions were trying to move him away from the will of God.

Let's examine how Jesus had victory over his emotions:

- He prayed

- He looked forward—Jesus thought about you and me and did what was right. He went beyond his emotions to consider the long term effects of his actions.

- He focused on the truth—Jesus chose the path of truth by lining himself up with the Word of God. He denied emotions that were against his will, purpose and mission.

Our emotions are not unique from the ones Jesus was struck with at the Garden of Gethsemane. He had victory over his emotions by living beyond them and submitting them to the Word of God. Jesus can absolutely relate to any feelings we might experience, and he can certainly make a way out for us.

Authority Over Emotions

Emotions cause bodily changes and behavioural reactions. For instance, a man who works with money every day might pursue the idea of taking some money one day when there is less supervision. He risks the chance of being fired for his actions because his emotions are leading him astray.

Indeed, emotions are needful for the progression of the universe. God gave us emotions that help us display compassion and goodness to each other. Furthermore, the devil perverts our emotions, since his number one weapon against the

Christian life is suggestion. The devil has no power towards Believers except through suggestion and deception. It is up to Believers to take hold of their spiritual authority against the works of the enemy.

Luke 10:19 reads:

I have given you authority to trample on snakes and scorpions and to overcome all the power of the enemy; nothing will harm you.

In the beginning, God give Adam authority to rule and reign over all creation, but Adam forfeited his spiritual authority to Satan. However, Jesus came to destroy the works of the devil (see John 10:10) and is now seated in the heavenly realm at the right hand of God the Father. Jesus has already stripped Satan of his authority and has given it to Believers. What are we doing with our spiritual authority? The Believer has power and authority over the power of the enemy—including where our emotions are concerned—and nothing shall by any means harm us.

The root of positive emotion is the Word of God. It's important to know who you are in Christ and the power of his resurrection. The root of negative emotion is a feeling of defencelessness. It's the feeling that there is no way out of a situation or circumstance. We have to make decisions based on the Word of God instead of basing them on our emotions. God does not want us to love him emotionally, but wholeheartedly.

Many obstacles in our lives are partly due to decisions we make based on our emotions. We tend to make emotional decisions without thinking and then end up facing the consequences in the long run. In addition, emotional love can only endure for a period of time since it's not based on a solid foundation like agape love. This kind of love can only stay active as long as the feeling still exists.

The degree to which you gain control of your emotions will be the degree to which you will control your life.

Your thinking will determine your emotions.

Your emotions will determine your decisions.

Your decisions will determine your actions.

Your actions will determine your habits.

Your habits will determine your character.

Your character ultimately will follow the pattern of your life.

If you can control your emotions,

You can control your words,

Your words will direct your life, and

You will eventually possess the abundant life!

Chapter 5

THE POWER OF WORDS

The tongue has the power of life and death, and those who love it will eat its fruit. (Prov. 18:21)

CHOOSE YOUR WORDS CAREFULLY

Words, faith and things work interchangeably. You cannot completely acquire faith without speaking words; likewise you cannot have things in your possession without having faith. Words are equal to things and things are equal to words. When we speak words, conception takes place and eventually images are transmitted. Our words have the ability to affect every part of us, including our immune system, nerves, brain, etc. Many today are eating the fruit of death due to the misuse of words. They have been trapped by their own words and become prisoners of fear and lack.

In the beginning, God spoke faith-filled *words* to create this universe, but now we see *images* of the things he spoke. We live in the manifestation of what God spoke. There's an old saying that "sticks and stones may break my bones but words will never kill me," but that's far from the truth—evidently words can trap, destroy and kill you.

We can frame our own world simply by the words that we use in our everyday lives. The words in our vocabulary can either prosper us or destroy us. The power of life and death that is carried by our tongue should not be underestimated.

God created us with four sets of ears: two inner ears and two outer ears. We hear ourselves through our inner ears while speaking, and the receiver hears us through their outer ears. Inner ears process words directly to the human heart or spirit. Your words have a bigger affect on your own health and life than on the person you are speaking to.

Control your tongue—don't let it control you!

It is absolutely vital to think before you speak, otherwise don't let any words proceed out of your mouth. Most often it is better for our actions to speak for us rather than saying silly random words. Words are one of the most powerful transmitters. They are able to transmit faith or fear depending on the usage.

The Power of Words

For example, one day I was getting directions from a certain friend to visit his house. As he was describing his neighbourhood and the type and colour of the house he lives in, I developed a mental image of it in my mind. When I finally got to the house, what I saw was the same as the image I had pictured in my mind. His words produced an image in my mind of something I had not seen before.

The Bible says in Prov. 18:7,

A fool's mouth is his undoing, and his lips are a snare to his soul.

We have authority over the tongue, so we shouldn't allow the tongue to control us. A fool's mouth is setting the course of his or her life. What words are you saying over your life?

How many futile words did you use in your vocabulary today? Watching over your words ultimately protects your life. God gave us his eternal Word for us to be able to speak his words after him. Any word that does not line up with the Word of God is evil. The Word of God is the will of God. God's Word is God's will. God's Word will produce faith and God's image inside of you. The devil's words will produce fear and the devil's image inside of you.

Whose words are you choosing? Grab a hold of your tongue and start speaking words of wisdom, power, prosperity, and knowledge.

Pleasant Words

Pleasant words are a honeycomb, sweet to the soul and healing to the bones. (Prov. 16:24)

Words are able to break one's heart or cheer one's heart. Pleasant words are very powerful; they can change situations and circumstances. It makes an enormous difference to use encouraging words to lift up the broken-hearted and the hopeless instead of using condemning words to make them feel worse. Our words are able to send healing power to a sick body. In Prov. 12:18 we read: "…the tongue of the wise brings healing." It's about time Christians started saying pleasant words over their health instead of complaining about their health. Let's use our words to bless our friends and family—and especially our children.

The Heart

Above all else, guard your heart, for it is the wellspring of life. (Prov. 4:23)

First of all, do we genuinely believe every word we say before we say it, whether good or bad, positive or negative, blessing or curse? The mouth's function is to say what has been registered in the heart. When we communicate, the words are already in our heart or making a connection to our mind. Those who say, "I can't do this," or, "I can do this," are both exactly right because they are saying what they believe in their heart. (When I refer to the heart I don't mean the one that pumps blood through your entire body, but the heart of your spirit.)

The human heart is the centre or the core of life. What goes inside the heart must come out from the heart. The things that go inside your heart are making your life. Thus, the heart cannot lie; it is the tongue that lies. It's amazing how you can listen to music in the morning and in the afternoon or evening your mouth will pick up the same song and you will start singing it again. What happens is that the words to the songs have been programmed into your heart or spirit. It's important to pay attention to what we listen to on TV, in music, and what we allow our ears to hear. We have to feed our spirit with the Word of God by listening to sermons, reading the Word, meditating on the Word, talking about the Word, etc.

The Bible says that God looks at a man's heart while people look at his outward appearance (1 Sam. 16:7). God knows that it is the heart that reveals a person's character. We are always quick to judge a book by its cover. We shouldn't criticize someone because of his or her appearance or cultural background; as a matter of fact, we should get to know them.

Heart Deception
James 1:26 says:

If anyone considers himself religious and yet does not keep a tight rein on his tongue, he deceives himself and his religion is worthless.

There are many Christians who are believing God for their breakthroughs with fasting and praying. When it seems like their prayers and confessions are not coming to pass due to afflictions, turmoil and trials, they give up and start making remarks about their prayers and confessions. However, our heart is like the soil and our words are the seeds. In the natural we cannot go back to dig up the pineapple seeds that were planted three weeks ago and start planting apple seeds—the harvest would be ineffective. Many hearts (soil) are confused due to the increased amounts of different seeds (words) that are being planted that should not be planted. The more we speak words that are contrary to what we believe in our heart, the more they will result in death over the situation instead of life. Your tongue can deceive your heart into thinking that the words you are speaking are what you want in your life.

The heart's function is to produce what you request. Some people have the courage to use any word they can find in the dictionary to describe how they feel at a particular time. For example, *I'm dying to go, I will die if I don't go; I laughed until I died; I almost froze to death.* All these words are being registered in your spirit that will deceive your heart and gradually come to pass. It won't happen instantly, but the more you continually use these words, the more opportunity there is for conception to eventually take place. Someone might say, "I don't understand why bad things are always happening to me," But nothing just happens out of nowhere. What happens in your life has a connection to the words you speak over your life.

Dominion over Words

Gen. 1:28 reads:

> *God blessed them and said to them, "be fruitful and increase in number; fill the earth and subdue it. Rule over the fish of the sea and the birds of the air and over every living creature that moves on the ground."*

God gave Adam the authority to rule and reign in the Garden of Eden, making all the living creatures subject to him. Adam took care of the Garden daily and named every living creature. God was God above the heavens and Adam was the god over the earth. Adam was capable of operating on the same level of faith as God, able to speak and command. He was another "speaking spirit" like God. Adam had the will power to speak creative words against the devil's deception in the Garden. Imagine what would have happened if he took advantage of his spiritual authority!

Most Christians today are just like Adam; they have neglected their power and authority to supply and demand things in this world. They have allowed the devil to take advantage of their will, mind and emotions.

James 3:2–5 reads:

> *We all stumble in many ways. If anyone is never at fault in what he says, he is a perfect man, able to keep his whole body in check. When we put bits into the mouths of horses to make them obey us, we can turn the whole animal. Or take ships as an example. Although they are so large and are driven by strong winds, they are steered by a very small rudder wherever the pilot wants to go. Likewise the tongue is a small part of the body, but it makes great boasts. Consider what a great forest is set on fire by a small spark.*

Just as the horse is controlled by a bit in its mouth and the ship is controlled by a small rudder, your body is also controlled by your mouth. Our words can defile our whole body. Our body does not have a mind of its own; it needs to be told what to do. There might be physical pains in your body, or you may be sick in bed, but don't be prompt to say how you feel—say what you want to have! In 1 Pet. 2:24 the Bible reminds us that *by the stripes of Jesus we are healed.* If you can say all the right things when all you see are the wrong things, you can keep your whole body in check. Your mouth will command your body to bring your words to pass. I want to challenge you to listen to the words that you speak and ask yourself if you really want them in your life. The Bible says, *"Let the weakling say, 'I am strong!'"* (Joel 3:10). You can change your present situation by the words that you speak.

Medical Doctor Dean Ornish, in his book *Love & Survival*, made a statement afters years of practice. He said that, even though there are drugs, surgery for illness, and well being, there is nothing else that has a greater impact on our quality of life than love and intimacy. His philosophy was that patients receive quicker recovery when love and support are coming from family and friends rather than the opposite. In addition, he argues that love and intimacy are a root cause of what makes us sick or well, what causes sadness or happiness, what makes us suffer or what leads to healing.

If there was such a medicine available, every doctor would be prescribing it for their patients!

GOD SPOKE WORDS!

God Almighty pre-existed before the creation of the universe. There is no origin of God since he is the originator. Theologians and scientists have conducted many years of research about God and his origin but they cannot agree on their conclusions.

Scientists will argue that God created the universe out of nothing. Biblically speaking, that's untrue—the beginning came from within God and then God moved outward as he created the heavens and the earth.

God said, *"Let there be Light,"* and light appeared. Light moved at the speed of 186,000 miles per second at the time of creation.

He used his words as containers for his faith. Words are like spiritual containers; they will either contain faith or fear. Notice, in the book of Genesis, God used his creative ability and spoke approximately *ten faith-filled words* for creation to begin. Afterwards, he rested on the seventh day. God's words are already filled with faith before he speaks them because he already believes in his words.

Eph. 5:1 reads:

Be imitators of God, therefore, as dearly loved children.

God has given us that same spiritual authority, but instead of hiring the kingdom of God in our lives, we hire the kingdom of darkness. We are so quick to say things that our five senses prompt us to say instead of obeying God's Word. God says, "Believing is seeing"; the world says, "Seeing is believing."

In the natural we understand that children are "copycats." They are able to imitate what they see the people in their lives—parents, siblings, basically anybody—doing. A child does not know any better, thus they learn by watching. God desires for us to imitate him and his ways of doing things just like a child would imitate their parents. God wants us to have faith in him and speak his words.

People have what they say because they had what they said when they said what they had already. In other words, they are not changing the situation by speaking God's Word; instead they are having faith in the present situation and speaking it.

Chapter 6

WHAT IS FAITH?

Now faith is being sure of what we hope for and certain of what we do not see. (Heb. 11:1)

The Word of God holds the only accurate definition of faith you will ever find anywhere in the world. Many religions possess their own kind of traditional faith and beliefs that have been set up for generations to follow, but in the Christian faith, we believe in one true God, the Creator of the heavens and the earth (Gen. 1:1).

There is an enormous difference between biblical faith, which is arrived at by believing in the scriptures, and just having faith in your husband, wife or children.

"Now" faith includes a present tense and a future tense. It is something that we believe with confidence and have assurance that we will see in the future. Everything that we hope for finds its substance in faith. But without hope there isn't any substance for faith to give birth to. *Substance refers to raw material.* It is the actual material that other things are derived from. (For instance, water is a raw material. We are able to make soft drinks and food from water, yet without water we would not be able to make them.) Our hope acts as a gateway to entering into the promises of God and the things we desire in our lives through the eye of faith. Faith works at all times like the law of gravity, but so many times we fail to operate in it. The word of faith is a law of God. It is a spiritual principle.

Rom. 12:3,

...in accordance with the measure of faith God has given you.

Everyone is entitled to the same measure of faith when they are born again, regardless of if they are to be a Pastor, an Evangelist, or an usher. The difference between my faith and your faith depends on the amount of time we spend with the Word of God. I can remember a movie that I watched in my teenage years, *Dangerous Minds*. It was about an English teacher who was responsible to teach a bunch of students who were rebellious and had no passion to learn. The teacher was quite confused about how she wanted to teach her class, but she decided to start the school year by giving all the students 100% as an average at the beginning of her class. Then it was up to the students to maintain that mark by studying.

Likewise, it is up to the believer to increase their faith by studying the Word of God, believing and saying what they believe.

The Bible says in Rom. 10:17, *"Consequently, faith comes from hearing the message, and the message is heard through the word of Christ."* The hearing of the Word of God produces faith. In other words, the more often we study the Word, mediate on the Word, and talk about the Word, the more it will allow us to reach a level where we will have enough confidence to believe for things in our lives.

WHAT FAITH IS NOT

Faith is not a magical concept that will bring all of our desires to pass. It is not a mental assent operated by our five senses. Faith is not a religion. It is not just a formula that Christians use, but it is a principle of God. Some people think that if they just say something 100 times a day, they will automatically have possession of that thing. That's not the whole truth of the matter, even though faith involves speaking.

Mark 11:23 reads:

I tell you the truth, if anyone says to this mountain, "Go throw yourself into the sea," and does not doubt in his heart but believes that what he says will happen, it will be done for him.

Speaking, then *subtracting the doubt* from your heart and *adding the belief* in your heart *equals the having*. Let's convert this formula for faith into a mathematical equation: $1 - 1 + 1 = 1$. We will always arrive at "one" unless we forget to subtract doubt. So now doubt becomes an enemy to our faith. I'm convinced that there is an easier way to defend against doubt than to merely not think about the problem or just think only positively about the problem. We have to hold on firmly to our faith and confidence in the Word. Despite any circumstance that surrounds us, we can know that our Lord will never leave us nor forsake us (Heb. 13:5–6).

Notice how faith has to be in two places in order for it to work—in your heart and in your mouth. When there is no faith in your heart, you can always speak faith into your heart. Likewise, when you possess faith in your heart already, then can you speak out your faith, and that's when it becomes a spiritual force or doubly enormous power.

Furthermore, the reciprocal of faith is fear. When faith is absent, fear will become present. Just like faith is a spiritual force of God, fear is a spiritual force of the devil. Faith will work proficiently on the positive side as well as the negative side. When we speak God's Word it will produce faith and God's image inside of us. Conversely, when we speak the devil's word it will produce fear and the devil's image inside of us.

HOW TO DEVELOP FAITH

In order for us to develop faith, it is very important for us to understand what faith is and what faith is not. We develop faith by abiding in the Word of God and operating on our standard level. For example, you can't go from 5-foot-2 to 7-foot-10 all of a sudden. We have to work with the tools we already possess and understand the do's and don'ts involved. It is a process; we have to watch over our words so that our heart will not be deceived. Moreover, we will not be able to believe God's Word if we can't first of all believe our own words. Since faith requires saying what we believe in our heart, we can't speak contrary to what is in our heart. Sometimes we go over the edge by expressing perverse speech or crooked speech that will eventually weaken our faith.

In Luke 17:6 Jesus did not increase the apostles' faith when they asked for an increase in faith. However, he showed them how to *develop* faith by speaking. It is not going to take 100% faith for all the mountains in our lives to be removed. But it will take just an effort of faith. God is not asking for too much faith but enough to get things going in our lives. We cannot base our faith on what God did for someone else.

The more we speak, the more we will believe, and the more we believe, the more we will speak until faith comes.

God's faithfulness endures forever—even when we remain unfaithful. According to Amos 3:7, God never does anything without declaring it first, and if you think about it, you hardly do anything without saying it first either. Before David became a king, God revealed it to the prophet Samuel. Also, before Jesus was born on the earth, God had already revealed it to the prophet Isaiah. God is watching over his Word in order to perform it; he releases his faith through words. Faith itself does not only reside in the heart, it must be spoken in order to perform. The Bible says faith without a corresponding action is dead. Faith always sees the end results.

EVERYTHING IS POSSIBLE BY FAITH

And without faith it is impossible to please God... (Heb. 11:6a)

Faith is a virtue that believers need to have at their disposal. Although God desires to do good on our behalf, our lack of faith prevents him from doing so. God is moved by an act of faith, for he is a faithful God. Everything in the kingdom of God and on earth was created by faith-filled words. The Bible says that *"by grace you have been saved, through faith"* (Eph. 2:8) and *"Abram believed the Lord, and he credited it to him as righteousness"* (Gen. 15:6). Likewise, our faith in God will cause us to have God's provision in our lives. The world says, "Seeing is believing," but with the Word of God, "Believing is seeing." We need faith, not for things that can be seen, but for the unseen in the spiritual realm. Faith is a way of life, so we must be strong to exercise our faith in the Lord. Our prayers, healing, and prosperity will not be able to work without faith. It is the master key to unlocking everything in the kingdom of God.

Chapter 7

FAITH THROUGH LOVE

For in Christ Jesus neither circumcision nor circumcision has any value. The only thing that counts is faith expressing itself through love. (Gal. 5:6)

The kingdom of God is operated by the faith of God, but faith will not work without the love of God because love is what activates faith to work. Without the love of God flowing in our lives, our faith will become short-circuited. It is sort of like trying to get to the other side of a city by car (faith) and the only possible way is over a bridge (love). One will never be able to cross to the other side without the bridge (love), even if one acquires a vehicle (faith).

Yet, like many others, we want to walk before we crawl by seeking faith first before the love of God.

Now, I'm not downplaying faith, but we have to put first things first in the order of how they operate. Since faith works, the devil wants to blind our love walk, which is the source of our faith, in order to prevent us from having what we say. It's not enough to say, "I have faith," if you do not have love, since your love walk always determines the outflow of your faith.

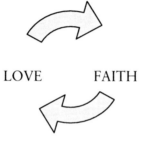

LOVE   FAITH

THE GREATEST THING IN THE WORLD

And now these three remain: faith, hope, and love. But the greatest is love. (1 Cor. 13:13)

For many centuries in the Christian circle, faith has been presumed as the masterpiece over love. Some say that faith is the most powerful thing in the universe today. But the Bible says that love is the greatest thing in the world. It is the very thing that we lack in the world, and the greatest thing we need today. There are wars and rumours of wars, poverty and division, all of which finds their roots in the lack of love. Love is the common resource for solving every problem, whether you believe it or not. Without the love of

God we will not be able to live beyond the problems that we face in this world today.

We hope for all the promises of God to work for us by faith through God's love, so we cannot have one without the other. Imagine what the world would be like today if nations and ethnic groups would unite together in love. I'm convinced that everyone knows how to love but they choose not to love. We have to pursue the way that will get us into the kingdom of God, and I believe when Jesus returns again it will not be about the greatest religion, the greatest race or culture, or the greatest faith, but the greatest love. The love we have for God and for our neighbours will be the most important.

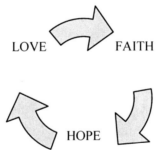

NO PROFIT

Everyone enters into a business with the intention of making a profit. Any business that is unable to produce any profit can no longer proceed. If a person spends millions of dollars on a business venture, only to come up with no profit at the end of the year, how devastating will that be?

When we analyze the scriptures, the apostle Paul defines the dialogue of love and its consequences on a similarly extreme level. God equipped the believers at Corinth with spiritual gifts for the purpose of edifying the church. Yet they became prideful, boastful, and arrogant and started to use those spiritual gifts for their own purposes instead of God's glory. Therefore, this caused division and dissension in the church. St. Paul goes on to explain what will happen to a person that has a spiritual gift without love:

> *If I speak in the tongues of men and of angels, but have not love, I am only a resounding gong or a clanging cymbal. (1 Cor. 13:1)*

The speaking of tongues is a heavenly language that some Christians use in their prayers. But the person who prays in tongues does not understand what they are saying, nor do the people who hear it. However, God understands it, for Paul says in 1 Cor. 14:2 that *anyone who speaks in a tongue does not speak to men but to God.*

I'm convinced that Paul was not making a reference to some Christians being able to speak angelic tongues. While he discusses the implications of being able to speak in humanly tongues and even having the ability to speak a high level of angelic tongue if possible, he stresses the higher importance of the fact that without love we are nothing but a resounding gong or a clanging cymbal. It's sort of like someone playing a musical instrument such as a drum but without any beat or rhythm being created.

> *If I have the gift of prophecy and can fathom all mysteries and all knowledge, and if I have a faith that can move mountains, but have not love, I am nothing. (1 Cor. 13:2)*

Secondly, St. Paul continues on to the superlative of the gifts of the spirit. He points out that even though one is embodied with the gift of prophecy that enables them to predict future events beyond measure and gives them an ability to comprehend the world's mysteries like no other, without love it profits that individual nothing. Notice how this person will be able to draw a crowd and the praise of men but not gain heavenly reward.

Moreover, he also contrasts faith and love once again. He goes on to say that even if one possess the greatest faith—to move mountains such as healing, financial prosperity—behold, without love that individual is a useless nobody.

> *If I give all I possess to the poor and surrender of body to the flames, but have not love, I gain nothing. (1 Cor. 13:3)*

Lastly, Paul discusses a person sowing seeds or offering their body as a sacrifice. For example, let's consider a man who is in possession of a large amount of the world's wealth. He can go around doing good to the mass majority of people, but without love it profits him nothing. That is because love has to be his motivation for those good works. Many times people have other motives for the things they do. As a matter of fact, good works will not be able to get anybody into the kingdom of God except through Christ Jesus.

Furthermore, Paul speaks of someone deliberately offering their body to be burned alive for the sake of another, but not having love. It profits them nothing. Nowadays, some people offer their organs—heart, kidneys, and even blood—for the sake of another; nevertheless, love has to be the motivating force behind these deeds, not money nor reward from men.

> *Love never fails. But where there are prophecies, they will cease; where there are tongues, they will be stilled; where there is knowledge, it will pass away. For we know in part and we prophesy in part, but when perfection comes, the imperfect disappears. (1 Cor. 13:8–10)*

As much as we desire spiritual gifts, they will not be able to work in their highest potential without love.

Chapter 8

TYPES OF LOVE

"Love" is used in the contexts of various aspects of life, such as families, friendships, love relationships, etc. Everybody wants to be loved by somebody, thus everyone needs love in their life. Ultimately, love is supreme and everlasting, and nothing else comes close to it.

In ancient Greek there are four words used for love, each with a different meaning: *Storge*, *Phileo*, *Eros*, and *Agape*. I'm convinced that these four types of love are necessary in every marriage in order to build a strong foundation. However, when any of these are absent, there will be a loophole in the relationship that will leave it unsuccessful. We will now collectively look at each of these areas more closely.

1. *Storge: "affectionate love between family members"*

The affection from a mother to a child is a reflection of *storge*. A mother's undivided attention is drawn to assisting her child at all times: during sickness, discomfort, crying, feeding, and most importantly, keeping warm. The mother's happiness comes from the child's health and well-being. Theoretically, she will sacrifice her life for that child's safety. *Storge* love is what children have towards their parents. It assures them that their parents will be present to their attention. Parents and children enjoy spending time with each other, participating in activities like reading, cycling, fishing, and playing sports. *Storge* love is also shared between extended family members, and most often it is taken for granted. In contrast to the other three loves, it is the closest to *agape* love in the sense that God is able to be tolerant with us, just like a mother is tolerant with her child. So many times, we see this type of affection amongst wildlife species. *Storge* binds families together and keeps a smooth relationship going at all times. The phrase *"blood is thicker than water"* is true in the affection that displays amongst most families when one member is sick or hurt or experiencing times of hardship.

> *When he was twelve, Jesus went with his parents to Jerusalem to attend the feast of the Passover. On their return to Nazareth, Mary and Joseph realized that their son was left behind. They anxiously searched for their son's whereabouts, and later discovered him at the*

temple sharing the Word of God with the teachers. (Luke 2:41–52)

During that time period the Jews were to go to Jerusalem every year to celebrate the Feast of the Passover. It was a day in the calendar year that was set as a memorial for the day the Lord delivered them from the hands of the Egyptians. Ideally, it was one of the most important and busiest days, similar to the month of December for us.

Upon their departure from Jerusalem Mary and Joseph discovered that their Son was not with them. Imagine the disappointment, concern, and fear they experienced while they anxiously searched for their son. I'm convinced that every parent would have reacted in the same manner, for it displays the love and the deeply rooted bond that families share.

2. Phileo: "friendship love"

Phileo is a broad word and it has many forms applied to it. Friendship can be formed for various reasons and its existence depends on the individuals involved. Friends are an excellent gift to acquire and a good friend is a great package to cherish. You have probably come across this phrase before: "Bad company corrupts good character."

In the world today, there are friends that stick closer than a brother; likewise, there are also friends that stick closer than an enemy. Certain individuals prefer friends that share in a common interest such as sports, school, or book clubs. However, the most important foundations to build on are trust and loyalty. Like many relationships, when trust and loyalty are evicted, a friendship slowly falls apart.

There has probably been a time in your life when you confided in a friend that you really trusted and they backstabbed you brutally. In my teenage years, I was emotionally depressed for being a kind hearted friend. A friend of mine had made up rumours about a certain individual and my name was mentioned. When given the opportunity to confront my friend, I refused, determining that whatever he said was said and done. I was reluctant to make friends again after learning that the hard way. With an anguished expression on my face, I asked myself, "Do I deserve all this?" There are always going to be ups and downs in relationships.

The uniqueness of friendship is that it acts as the key entry door to any further intimate relationship for the simple fact that it provides the opportunity to get to know your mate's personality. Maybe you will discover that this is not the relationship you want to be involved in.

In light of this, the qualities of *storge* are seldom noticeable between two individuals that have developed a friendship over a period of time. Most often, in *phileo*, friends share ideas and relate to each other's opinions.

David and Jonathan developed their friendship to the point that they made a covenant before the Lord to protect each other forever. The Bible says Jonathan became one spirit with David and loved him as himself. Now there's an instance of *agape* love being displayed alongside *phileo* love. Affectionate friendship is essential in a marriage relationship in order to excel to a higher horizon. However, to make friends is not the same as to build an affectionate relationship. As a good friend of mind says, *"a friend that cares is a friend indeed."*

3. Eros: "romantic love; sexual desires"

In Greek mythology, Eros was known as the god of lust, love, and sexuality. There is a great mystery behind the origination of Eros in the world of mythology, and he is often portrayed as an angel that carries a bow with heart shaped arrows and has a halo above his head. In this passage, however, I'm more concerned about the meaning of the word than its relationship with historical events.

Eros is the beautiful feeling that occurs when two lovers develop their desires for each other. It often includes expressing your feelings freely to each other by doing things together such as romantic dinners, walks in the park, or just simply spending quality time together. On occasions such as Valentine's Day, it allows the opportunity for lovers to embrace each other. A warm hug and a kiss will probably say much more than a dozen roses, chocolates or candies. *Eros* could be the one thing that you love or appreciate about your mate.

We see in the scriptures that Adam and Eve shared and experienced *eros* love together. God commanded them to be *"fruitful and increase in number."* It is God's special idea for a husband and wife to exploit *eros* love in a marriage relationship. Romantic love or sexual desire for your lover is not necessarily wrong as long as it is within the context of marriage.

4. Agape Love – *"unconditional or selfless love for others"*

Agape love ranks the highest in comparison with the other loves. Somehow, it is the hardest one to detect in the world today. Without this type of love operating in a relationship it will eventually cause *storge*, *phileo*, and *eros* loves to become ineffective. Most marriages end up in a divorce court because the partners don't want to sacrifice their lives for each other. A marriage that is built on agape love will be able to stand the rain, the storms, and the pressures of life.

LOVE AND MARRIAGE

I am the vine; you are the branches. If a man remains in me and I in him, he will bear much fruit; apart from me you can do nothing. (John 15:5)

Now here is a powerful scripture that Jesus wants us to understand and hold in our heart. So many times, couples believe they have everything figured out in their marriage—they have good jobs that bring home a good income, they have a beautiful home and a luxurious car, and they have earned respect from their peers and society—but just wait until they encounter serious marital conflicts. That's when they seek for marital mayday. Let's understand that anything other than the hand of God will only cover the surface of marital conflicts; only God is the antidote to all these problems. When couples are able to employ God's ways by praying and compromising it will be able to save their relationship from going into the marital graveyard.

The Bible lets us know that the two will become one flesh after they have united in marriage (Eph 5:31). For this reason a husband and wife ought to empathize with each other. It is not about "me" but about "us." In every successful marriage there is a fabric of trust, love and forgiveness. And if couples are able to overlook certain things and have frequent peace talks over matters, then there will be a happy marriage. On the other hand, hostile words such as these will promote problems:

- "Oh, why did you leave your clothes in the living room?"

- "Do you remember when I cleaned up after your mess?"
- "You forgot about our anniversary last year!"
- "Well, guess what, you forgot about my birthday!"

Sometimes—let me rephrase that—*all* the time it benefits couples to flashback to the day they stood before the altar and made vows to each other and, most importantly, to God. It seems to have been forgotten on the journey of marriage. One of the most famous ceremonial decrees exchanged by marriage couples is as follows:

> "I, ( )
> Take you, ( )
> To be my (wife/husband),
> To have and to hold,
> For better, for worse,
> For richer, for poorer,
> In sickness and in health,
> To love and to cherish,
> Till death do us part"

Whatever happened to the *phileo* love before and after the trip to the altar? Or maybe there is not enough *eros*, even though it is not the centre of marital solution. Whatever happened to *agape* love, which creates peace, not war; love, not hate; happiness, not sorrow?

Types of Love

Love is not just saying a bunch of "I love you" words, it proceeds with action. The Bible says that faith without corresponding actions is dead. Likewise, love without corresponding actions is also dead. When one spouse is able to overlook their partner's faults and weakness, God will provide the necessary tools for the other spouse to change. It is of no use to complain all the time without making any changes.

One of the most effective changes one can make in a marriage is to change oneself. It is not fair for one spouse to demand the other to change, since the detrimental faults might be from the spouse that is demanding the change. Better yet, it would be an excellent common practice for both parties to compromise, as the root cause of every dysfunctional marriage seems to be based on the absence of *agape* love. *Agape* love brings enjoyment and flavour into a marriage.

Chapter 9

JESUS, OUR EXAMPLE

There is no one perfect but the one who has walked on this earth without sin—Jesus Christ, the Son of the Living God. As a matter of fact, we cannot claim to be perfect or close to perfection without being taught about the one who has paved the way for a lost world. Our Lord Jesus, who came to show the Way to the world and give ultimate meaning to life, resides in heaven today. Meanwhile, as it was in the past so it holds true in this present time, some raise questions about Jesus, asking, "Is he a man with great credentials? . . . or a prophet with divine powers?" Well, the answer to both questions is exactly right.

The life of Christ and his contemporaries is greatly highlighted in the first four books of the New Testament, the Gospels: Matthew, Mark, Luke and John. Jesus was rejected, arrested, and crucified for the redemption of mankind. During his ministry he taught a lot using parables, sermons, illustrations, and examples to compare natural and spiritual things. Our duty as Christians is to carry on the legacy of Christ Jesus to the world. In the world of religion it can sometimes get complicated with the competition, comparison and the differences attached to it.

THE GOOD SHEPHERD

I am the good shepherd. The good shepherd lays down his life for the sheep. (John 10:11)

What a friend we have in Jesus, who laid his life down at all costs for the sake of his sheep, unlike an ordinary shepherd who will flee for their life and thereby put the sheep in danger for intruders to devour. The Psalmist understood the importance of the Lord being the shepherd over his life in order to experience the abundant life God promised. He proclaimed it over his life: *"The Lord is my Shepherd, I shall not be in want"* (Ps. 23:1).

David lived the life of a shepherd during his early years and didn't need anyone to convince him of the magnificence of such a statement. He understood the basic daily needs of his sheep and how to keep them protected from predators. With that insight in mind, he was fully persuaded that if God became his shepherd he would not lack anything, like the sheep under his care. Like typical sheep, always wandering away from the flock and unable to survive without their shepherd, so it is true with Christians. As much as the shepherd desires to lead all his sheep to their gate, apparently, not all of them will be able to make it.

The person that is fully persuaded that the Lord is their shepherd will not fear or lack anything. They are able to wait upon the Lord with patience, unlike other sheep that stop going to church when trouble comes or that lose faith in their shepherd, the one who is able to save them.

THE GOOD SAMARITAN (LUKE 10:25–37)

On one occasion an expert in the law stood up to test Jesus. "Teacher," he asked, "what must I do to inherit eternal life?"

"What is written in the Law?" he replied. "How do you read it?"

He answered: "'Love the Lord your God with all your heart and with all your soul and with all your strength and with all your mind'; and, 'Love your neighbor as yourself.'"

"You have answered correctly," Jesus replied. "Do this and you will live."

But he wanted to justify himself, so he asked Jesus, "And who is my neighbor?"

Jesus makes it clear that we can become a Good Samaritan to everyone, including our enemies. So often we tend to give a short hand to the opportunity that lies ahead of us by neglecting to reach out to one another. In this parable, a certain man was beaten, wounded, and left unattended by robbers. Along came a Priest, but he passed by without reaching out to him. Meanwhile, a Levite came across the victim and also walked past him without stopping. Finally, a Samaritan man was travelling on that path when he noticed the lifeless body lying on the roadside. He quickly tended to the body and raced the victim to the hospital. After Jesus had enlightened the expert of the Law with this parable, he returned the question to him, saying:

> *"Which of these three do you think was a neighbor to the man who fell into the hands of robbers?"*
>
> *The expert in the law replied, "The one who had mercy on him."*
>
> *Jesus told him, "Go and do likewise."*

There's a great lesson behind this parable that we can utilize in our everyday lives. When we examine the individuals that approached this man who fell into the hands of the robbers, one would stress that the Priest should have been the first person to attend to the victim. Thus it was the least likely of them all who showed the best example of love. At that point in history, Jews and Samaritans held a deep hatred towards each another, but this Samaritan man disregarded the division between them and stopped to help his enemy. According to Jesus, this man demonstrated an act of love to his neighbour and to God.

Chapter 10

DIVINE LOVE

For it is by grace you have been saved, through faith—and this not from yourselves, it is the gift of God. (Eph. 2:8)

God's love is the "crown of life and the school of virtue." It endures forever, shed abroad from far ends of the world, and it remains consistently the same. Henceforth, we have to leave behind the world's ways of loving each another and attend to the school of virtue. I have made up my mind to attend and graduate from that school, and I hope you feel the same.

One of the greatest gifts God has given to mankind is both a Need-Gift and a Free-Gift. We were in need of salvation and God gave us his only begotten son to die for our iniquities—Need-Gift. Our duty is to receive this gift by believing and confessing his son's name—Free-Gift (Rom. 10:9–10). It is not a complicated concept, but somehow many find it difficult to receive.

Apparently, we didn't have to do anything to earn this precious gift; otherwise, it wouldn't be grace at all. It came as a result of God's grace. Grace is God's unmerited favour; that is, God doing something for us that we don't deserve. The grace of God is the love of God in action. Isa. 30:18 reads:

Yet the Lord longs to be gracious to you; he rises to show you compassion. For the Lord is a God of justice.

We know and understand that a hungry person's remedy will consist of an answer to their need of food. Conversely, a thirsty person's remedy will be an answer to their need of water. Likewise, our Heavenly Father understands that we will be in a need of certain things while here on earth. He has made a provision, so that we may receive our Need-Gift by asking him.

I speak for myself, and hopefully for everybody, when I say we all love to receive free gifts. So many times we hear people say that *"there's nothing free in this world."* Well, that not the whole truth, because God's love is free, and it will free you to love others. It comes with no strings attached, unlike human love.

Isa. 55:7 reads:

Let the wicked forsake his way and the evil man his thoughts. Let him turn to the Lord, and he will have mercy on him, and to our God, for he will freely pardon.

This Free-Gift of salvation applies to every person on the face of the planet. God is not concerned about your sins, but he is certainly concerned about you receiving his Free-Gift. You might feel unworthy, guilty, or sinful, but God's arms are ready to receive you. Better yet, God does not send people to hell. It is when people neglect to receive their Need-Gift and Free-Gift that they position themselves in that direction.

God our Father, the maker of the heavens and the earth, is greater than all the sub-gods in the world. Many gods have come and have passed on in life, but Almighty God lives forevermore. One is able to observe in society an aspect of God's love that is unique in nature and common to all humanity, something which theologians classify as "common grace." We see how both the righteous and the unrighteous benefit from the experience of inhaling and exhaling of oxygen through their bodies. Furthermore, both also benefit from a glass of water or a fresh piece of fruit as an act of God's grace. Notice, both enjoy the usage of natural resources. However, God does not owe us anything in advance, but his unfailing love is lavished on the vast majority.

ABOUNDING GRACE

The Lord is not slow in keeping his promise, as some understand slowness. He is patient with you, not wanting anyone to perish, but everyone to come to repentance. (2 Pet. 3:9)

Although God is love, we must understand that the degree of God's love is somehow limited for the unrighteous but unlimited for the righteous. This first condition is arrived at by rejecting to acquire the Need-Gift and Free-Gift, while the second is for those who practice the Word of God. God has promised a final destination for both individuals according to their conduct. Like a double-edged sword, God is love while also being the judge of the living and the dead.

It is vitally important for us to gain understanding concerning the other attributes of God. God is a God of vengeance and he is our Judge, but this does not limit his authority, power, dignity, or sovereignty, nor do these attributes by any means isolate God from his character of love. For instance, a nonbeliever will not be able to enter the kingdom of God. Just like water and oil cannot mix but remain separated, likewise God is holy and naturally separate from sinners. One might say that this is unfair of God. However, what would be unfair would be God not providing a way for us to enter his kingdom.

When a teacher of a class deliberately decides to give an examination without the students' knowledge that is unfair. Why? Because the students were not aware of the teacher's actions. But that is not our case. God has given unto men his son as atonement for sin and sixty-six books of Gospel that outline the future of the universe. We possess the power to determine what happens in our lives.

God and Parents

I'm convinced that every parent would put two thumbs up to agree that raising children is not an easy process. Some parents find success at it while others tend to abandon their children. However, every parent desires the best that life has to offer for their offspring. For instance, they want their children to attend the best school to get educated so they can get a better job and also a better life. Sometimes, however, things may not turn out the way they desire them to be.

Children value their parents' attention, time and love, for it gives them a sense of security. The way a child is raised will be reflected in his or her adult life as well. It is said, *"charity begins at home,"* and that discipline is the key for raising a rebellious child. Discipline is not necessarily spanking, punishing, or abusing a child. Some parents set up rules and regulations for their kids and when these are violated they lose certain privileges. It is pretty clear that all these things that parents do are for their children's security and welfare even though they may not understand.

God is the father of us all, and he desires far better for his children than what a human parent has to offer. Our limited understanding is unable to comprehend the love of God for us. The Bible says in Eph. 3:19 that God's love *surpasses knowledge*. I believe that's the reason why we feel as if God is trying to take all the fun in the world away from us. Just like a parent instructs and protects their children so they won't be led astray, that's what God is doing on our behalf.

Once upon the time, there was a little boy named Johnny who fell in love with a hamster. The hamster was never left unattended as the boy took it to school, church, bed, and practically everywhere he went. It was probably taken care of far better then other pets. Johnny would cry to his parents when the pet was sick and smile when the pet was well. When Johnny's parents took the pet away from him, they discovered that it was contaminated with a disease. Johnny's parents didn't know how to confront him, for he was too young to understand. Meanwhile, little Johnny cried every day for his hamster to come back. I believe that Johnny was upset with his parents for taking his hamster away from him, but his parents assured him that they loved him and don't want any harm in his life.

The love that Johnny's parents had for him caused them to take the hamster away from him. As a result of the agape love that God has for his children, he sent Jesus to destroy the works of the devil so his children would not be in bondage to sin but free from sin. God's love for us is not only more significant than that of a parent, but immeasurable and supreme.

God's Creation

The greatest virtue that connects us in perfect unity in heaven or on earth is the love of God. We all have something to be thankful about, whether directly or indirectly. It would be an act of selfishness to deny the goodness of God within our circles. How vast is the sum of God's creation? Notice the earth in which we dwell, how it's spins on its axis every twenty-four hours, yet we don't observe any objects moving around us. The sun, with its energy driven nature, impacts the earth. The lilies of the fields blossom. It is a wonder to watch the moving from season to season and time to time. We all experience the beauty of God's creation in different ways.

> *Let them give thanks to the Lord for his unfailing love and his wonderful deeds for men. (Ps. 107:15)*

"SPIRIT DIVINE, COME DOWN"

Conclusion

MINDSET

I have heard some people say, "Change your mind," or, "Make up your mind," since we possess the deciding factor and no one else has that power.

Our mind plays an enormous role in terms of our decision-making. It is absolutely impossible for one to know everything that goes on in another's mind (unless you are God). However, a person is able to influence another's mindset.

When I was growing up, my parents used to repeatedly recite to me and my sisters that we could become whatever it was that we desired to become, but only if we put our minds to it. I'm convinced that every one of us probably heard this statement one way or the other while growing up. I wondered, *"What is it about the mind involvement that will actually get the job accomplished?"* I came to the conclusion that when we set our minds on a certain thing we are relentlessly impacted by perseverance to achieve our destination.

The same is true when we become newborn in Christ Jesus. Although we have become a new breed and the old things are passed away and substituted with a new life, it still comes down to the individual changing their mindset in order to develop a right action. By any means, if we attempt to change our actions prior to developing a right mindset, we will ultimately fail in the process.

It is of utmost importance for us to set our minds and keep them set on the things we desire. As far as this book is concerned, it will take a determined attitude in order to develop a godly character. It is absolutely great for us to acquire knowledge, but it is of no use when we don't put it into practice. It is going to take more than a day or two for us to develop an excellent character, but when we make an effort, God will get involved to help us through. As humans, we are a product of what we think in our minds. For instance, if you think you can never live an abundant life, consequently it will not happen for you, and vice versa. A defeated mindset will stay defeated until you turn the switch around.

The power of the mind cannot be understated as day in and day out our minds are filled with millions of things that are not valuable to us. It is time that we challenge our subconscious mind, for the mind is a terrible thing to waste. In spite of all these challenges bombarding us, the Bible makes it clear that we can renew our minds with the Word of God (Rom. 12:2). The more often we study, meditate, and listen to the Word, the more it will eventually dictate our minds.

Selected References

The American Heritage Student Dictionary. (Boston: Houghton Mifflin, 1986

Capps, Charles. *The Tongue, A Creative Force.* (Tulsa: Harrison House, 1995).

The Life Application Study Bible NIV. (Carol Stream, IL: Tyndale House, 1997).

Dollar, Creflo A. Jr. "Emotions" sermon series. (www.creflodollarministries.org).

Dollar, Creflo A. Jr. "Love: The Greatest Commandment" sermon series. (www.creflodollarministries.org).

Dollar, Creflo A. Jr. *The Color of Love: Understanding God's Answer to Racism, Separation, and Division.* (Tulsa: Harrison House, 1997).

Evans, Dylan. *Emotions: A Very Short Introduction.* (New York: Oxford University Press, 2003).

Lewis, C. S. *The Four Loves.* (Glasgow: William Collins, 1960) 111.

Ornish, Dr. Dean, MD. *Love & Survival: The Scientific Basis for the Healing Power of Intimacy*, Large print edition. (Waterville, ME: Thorndike Press, 1998).

Radicliffe, J. *The New International Webster's Pocket Dictionary of the English Language.* (Naples, FL: Trident Reference Publishing, 1997).

ABOUT THE AUTHOR

AKWASI AFRIYIE currently resides in Ontario, Canada, and is the third born of four siblings, originally from a town called Antoa in Ghana, West Africa. A graduate in the field of business insurance, his passion for God and the Word preached by admired influential Pastors and Bible teachers inspired him to accomplish this book. In his leisure time, he enjoys writing stories and poems as well as giving back to his community. He is described by peers and family members as a compassionate and easy-going individual, and some of his aspirations include becoming a motivational speaker and helping to spread the Gospel.

Printed in the United States
129455LV00005B/2/P